MAD

ABOUT

SPORTS

by Frank Jacobs

Illustrated by
Jack Rickard

with a
Guest Appearance
by Don Martin

Edited by
Albert B. Feldstein

with a Foreword by
Nick Meglin

WARNER BOOKS

A Warner Communications Company

Y0-CZO-439

CONTENTS

FOREWORD

By Nick Meglin

Before one can write with accuracy and insight on a subject such as Sports, one must experience first-hand what he is writing about. I can safely say that there is no writer more qualified to write "Mad About Sports" than Frank Jacobs. I can also safely say that no illustrator can equal Jack Rickard's intense interest in athletics. Rather than go on endlessly, allow me to use this space to list their accomplishments, not as literary men, but as *sportsmen*.

FRANK JACOBS
(1947-1964)[1]

Second-place winner, Marv Throneberry Golf Classic, 1962;[2] founder and past president of The Friends of Howard Cosell; seventeenth-round draft choice, Lincoln (Nebr.) Cougars, 1965.[3]

JACK RICKARD
(1868-   )[4]

Golden Gloves Eastern Championship, 1935;[5] second-place winner, Walt Dropo Masters, 1944;[6] winner of Roger Maris Asterisk Award, 1960.[7]

---

1 Frank is an occultist who believes he died in 1964 and was reincarnated back into his own body inasmuch as it was the finest specimen available at the time.

2 His caddy placed first.

3 A pinball team.

4 Jack is alive and well and living in the Astrodome with his lovely wife, Frances, and two children.

5 Overweight Division.

6 Tournament cancelled because of World War II.

7 Awarded to any athlete capable of eating 61 Baby Ruth candy bars while reading a 162-game baseball schedule.

THE MAD SPORTS HERO PRIMER

HERO

Chapter 1

See the Baby.
He is only six weeks old.
His Father calls him his "First-Round Draft Choice."
This is because he has decided
That the baby will grow up to be a Professional Athlete
And make a lot of money.
His Father took the first step the day his baby was born.
He named him Jock.

Chapter 2

See Jock at one year.
He says "Wagga goo blah-blah."
His Father is preparing him for life.
He is teaching him to blitz, and to tackle
And to pummel his teddy bear.
When Jock is five he will have learned
To do all these things.
And he will still be saying "Wagga goo blah-blah."

Chapter 3

See Jock run.

He is now seven.

He no longer says "Wagga goo blah-blah."

He says "Wagga goo blah-blah, Daddy."

But he has lightning speed, quick reflexes
And excellent physical coordination.

Which means he is toilet-trained.

His Father still wants him to be a
Professional Athlete.

But not a dumb Professional Athlete.

Therefore, he is encouraging Jock to read.

Today Jock was bought his first Children's Book.

In order to improve his mind.

The name of the book is
"The Roly-Poly Puppy Meets Bubba Smith."

Chapter 4

See Jock play High-School Football.
He is now 16 years old, is in superb physical
Condition, and is a Functional Illiterate.
He owes his skills to his Parents.
Thanks to their encouragement, he has become
The Complete Competitor.
He can run, block, kick, pass and maim.

See Jock at College.
In order to get him for its Football Team,
The College waived certain requirements.
Namely the Entrance Examination.
Jock is majoring in Creative Brooding.
Jock also works at an Off-Campus Job
Which the Athletic Department selected for him.
The job is as a Zeppelin Spotter.

See the Big College Game.
Jock is up for the Game.
No, he did not get a Pep Pill from the Trainer.
Jock is up for the Game because he knows
There are Pro Scouts in the stands.
A Scout from the Rams wants him as a Line-Backer.
A Scout from the Packers wants him as a Tackle.
A Scout from the Mafia wants him as a Hired Killer.
Jock now weighs 260 and has mastered
The Defensive Arts of Football.
He is proving it now on the field.
He is digging his cleats into the face
Of the opposing team's quarterback.
This is a very effective defensive move.
Especially since the game hasn't started yet.

Chapter 7

See Jock with the Pro Scout.
He is surrounded by his Advisors.
These include his Parents, his Lawyer,
His Business Advisor and his Keeper.
Jock's pro contract calls for a bonus of
$100,000, a yearly salary of $50,000,
Plus $5,000 for every time he destroys
A vital organ of an opposing player.
Jock is dissatisfied with the Contract.
He is a Hold-Out.
He is unhappy because there is no provision
For Raw Meat and Cornflakes at the Training Table.
Jock will get them, however, because
He has all The Skills.
Now all that remains is for Jock to okay
His name on the Contract.
This merely entails Jock signing his name.
Hmmm.
This was One Skill the Pro Scout didn't scout.
It looks like Jock is still a Hold-Out.

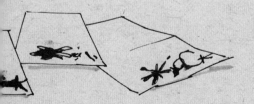

Chapter 8

See Jock in his first Pro Game.
He finally signed his contract.
By painstakingly copying the signature
On his Cornflakes Box.
Jock is now known as W. K. Kellogg.
But down deep he is still Jock.
Hitting, ramming, punching.
Crippling a defenseless punter.
Smashing the kidney of a fallen flanker.
Fracturing the shoulder of an NBC cameraman.
You may be wondering something.
Considering his superb physical condition,
You may be wondering how Jock avoided the Army.
The explanation is simple.
The Army passed up Jock when they
Learned that he was unable to serve
For a personal reason.
Namely, he is a Pacifist.

Chapter 9

See Jock at the Peak of his Career.
He has been named All-Pro for
The Fifth Consecutive Year.
He earns $85,000 a year.
He makes tons of Extra Money by endorsing
Razor Blades, Farm Tractors, Dog Food,
Atomic Reactors, Wind Tunnels, Bird Baths,
Seismographs and Industrial Asbestos.
But do not think that Jock lacks Integrity.
He would never endorse a product that he
Did not use personally.

Chapter 10

See Jock with the Pro Football Commissioner.
The Commissioner is chewing out Jock.
He believes Jock's business affairs are
Making Pro Football look too commercialized.
The Commissioner has a point.
After all, if every player behaved like Jock,
The Game might soon become merely
A Money-Making Machine.
After Jock leaves, the Commissioner
Will confer with a TV Network
About how much the Network will pay for
Six TV games on Sunday.
And three TV games on Monday.
And Highlights of Sunday's games on Tuesday.
And Highlights of Tuesday's Highlights on
Wednesday and Thursday.
And a Two-Hour Preview of next Sunday's
Games on Friday.
And how to get rid of College Football on Saturday.
Then the Commissioner will get down to his Main Point.
How to add an eighth day to the week.

Chapter 11

See Jock today.
Wait a minute. This can't be Jock.
Yes it is. He has retired at his peak.
He is worth a cool million and is set for life.
And now he is paying back Pro Football
For all that The Game has given him.
He has written a book revealing what a Rotten,
Degrading Business it all is.
His book has a clever title.
It is called "Football Stinks."
In his book Jock makes Startling Revelations.
That his Teammates play for Money.
That Locker Rooms smell after a game.
That Vietnam was a tragic mistake.
That the Environment is polluted.
That Existentialism is outmoded.
That Science is unyielding to the Arts.
That Einstein was wrong.
Gosh,
And to think some people still say
That Football is just a stupid game.

The Mad
HALL OF FAME
FOR
MINOR
SPORTS

SESSUE (ACE) FUJIMOTO

YOYO MASTER

FIRST PRO TO PLAY "MELANCHOLY BABY" ON
A SINGING DUNCAN, 1947. INTRODUCED
"FUJIMOTO TRIPLE," 1955, WHEREBY PLAYER
SIMULTANEOUSLY "WALKS THE DOG" UTILIZING
RIGHT HAND, LEFT HAND AND NOSE.
STRANGLED ON OWN STRING, 1958.

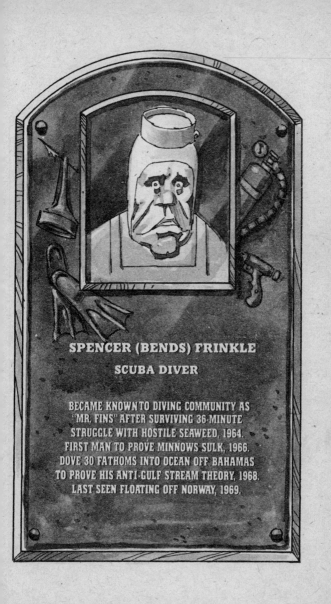

SPENCER (BENDS) FRINKLE

SCUBA DIVER

BECAME KNOWN TO DIVING COMMUNITY AS
"MR. FINS" AFTER SURVIVING 36-MINUTE
STRUGGLE WITH HOSTILE SEAWEED, 1964.
FIRST MAN TO PROVE MINNOWS SULK, 1966.
DOVE 30 FATHOMS INTO OCEAN OFF BAHAMAS
TO PROVE HIS ANTI-GULF STREAM THEORY, 1968.
LAST SEEN FLOATING OFF NORWAY, 1969.

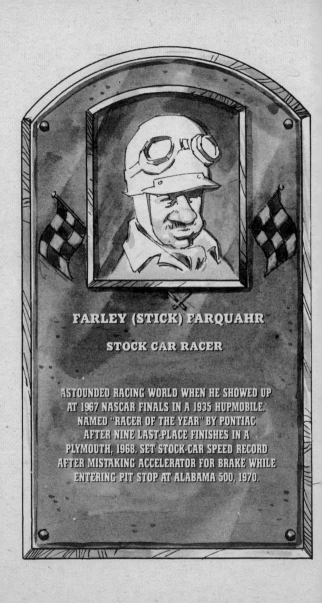

FARLEY (STICK) FARQUAHR

STOCK CAR RACER

ASTOUNDED RACING WORLD WHEN HE SHOWED UP
AT 1967 NASCAR FINALS IN A 1935 HUPMOBILE.
NAMED "RACER OF THE YEAR" BY PONTIAC
AFTER NINE LAST-PLACE FINISHES IN A
PLYMOUTH, 1968. SET STOCK-CAR SPEED RECORD
AFTER MISTAKING ACCELERATOR FOR BRAKE WHILE
ENTERING PIT STOP AT ALABAMA 500, 1970.

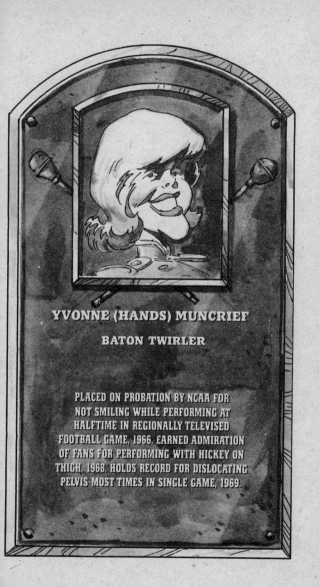

YVONNE (HANDS) MUNCRIEF

BATON TWIRLER

PLACED ON PROBATION BY NCAA FOR
NOT SMILING WHILE PERFORMING AT
HALFTIME IN REGIONALLY TELEVISED
FOOTBALL GAME, 1966. EARNED ADMIRATION
OF FANS FOR PERFORMING WITH HICKEY ON
THIGH, 1968. HOLDS RECORD FOR DISLOCATING
PELVIS MOST TIMES IN SINGLE GAME, 1969.

ZOLTAN ZANDAR

BICYCLE RACER

FIRST CYCLIST TO RIDE A 10-SPEED ATALA
RACER WITH ARMS FOLDED WITHOUT SHOUTING,
"LOOK MA, NO HANDS!" WON "PEDALER OF
YEAR" AWARD FOR HAVING ONLY SEVEN CYCLES
STOLEN WHILE LIVING IN NEW YORK CITY, 1968.
DEVOURED BY COYOTES WHILE ATTEMPTING TO
CROSS MEXICAN BAJA ON A SCHWINN TRAINER, 1971.

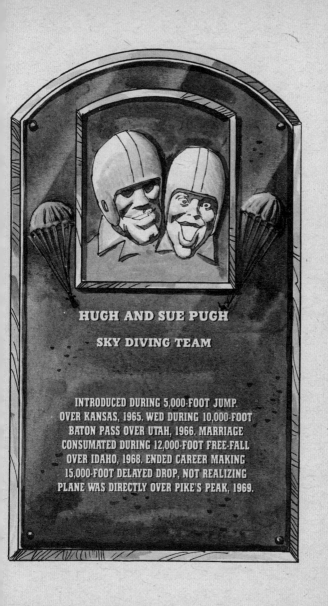

HUGH AND SUE PUGH

SKY DIVING TEAM

INTRODUCED DURING 5,000-FOOT JUMP
OVER KANSAS, 1965. WED DURING 10,000-FOOT
BATON PASS OVER UTAH, 1966. MARRIAGE
CONSUMATED DURING 12,000-FOOT FREE-FALL
OVER IDAHO, 1968. ENDED CAREER MAKING
15,000-FOOT DELAYED DROP, NOT REALIZING
PLANE WAS DIRECTLY OVER PIKE'S PEAK, 1969.

PHILO (SLAM) GULLGREED

PING PONG PLAYER

INVENTOR OF "BOOMERANG SERVE," WHEREBY
BALL BOUNCES ON OPPONENT'S SIDE, THEN
RETURNS TO STRIKE SERVER IN EYE, 1969.
ONLY U.S. PLAYER REQUESTED NOT TO RETURN
TO RED CHINA, 1971. RETIRED BECAUSE OF
INJURIES SUSTAINED WHEN LEAPING OVER
NET TO CONGRATULATE OPPONENT, 1972.

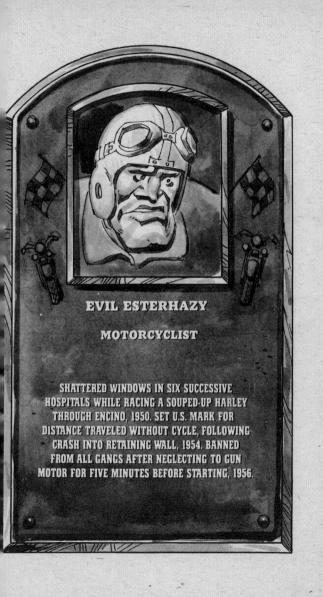

EVIL ESTERHAZY

MOTORCYCLIST

SHATTERED WINDOWS IN SIX SUCCESSIVE
HOSPITALS WHILE RACING A SOUPED-UP HARLEY
THROUGH ENCINO, 1950. SET U.S. MARK FOR
DISTANCE TRAVELED WITHOUT CYCLE, FOLLOWING
CRASH INTO RETAINING WALL, 1954. BANNED
FROM ALL GANGS AFTER NEGLECTING TO GUN
MOTOR FOR FIVE MINUTES BEFORE STARTING, 1956.

BROCK SCHLOCK

TUG-OF-WAR PLAYER

OVERCAME HANDICAP OF SWEATY PALMS TO
ANCHOR U.S. TEAM TO WORLD TITLE IN 1937.
ENTERED PROFESSIONAL RANKS, 1938. RETURNED
TO AMATEUR RANKS, 1939, AFTER DISCOVERING
NON-EXISTENCE OF PROFESSIONAL RANKS.
RETIRED AFTER MATCH IN AKRON, 1940, WHEN
ROPE SNAPPED, RECOILING HIM INTO CINCINNATI.

BORIS MANKOFF

CHESS MASTER

INVENTED "BUDAPEST OPENING," WHEREBY MOVE
OF KING'S BISHOP'S PAWN IS FOLLOWED BY
RIGHT CROSS TO OPPONENT'S CHIN. PLAYED
160 OPPONENTS SIMULTANEOUSLY WHILE CROSSING
STREET IN WARSAW, 1929. HOLDS RECORD FOR
LONGEST THOUGHT BETWEEN MOVES, IN
MATCH BEGUN IN MOSCOW, 1931, AND STILL CONTINUING.

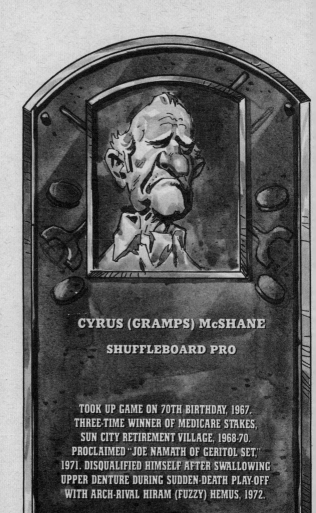

CYRUS (GRAMPS) McSHANE

SHUFFLEBOARD PRO

TOOK UP GAME ON 70TH BIRTHDAY, 1967.
THREE-TIME WINNER OF MEDICARE STAKES,
SUN CITY RETIREMENT VILLAGE, 1968-70.
PROCLAIMED "JOE NAMATH OF GERITOL SET,"
1971. DISQUALIFIED HIMSELF AFTER SWALLOWING
UPPER DENTURE DURING SUDDEN-DEATH PLAY-OFF
WITH ARCH-RIVAL HIRAM (FUZZY) HEMUS, 1972.

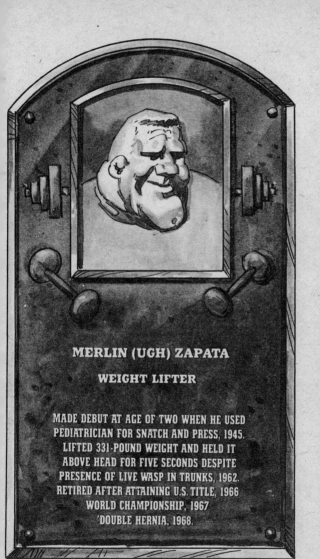

MERLIN (UGH) ZAPATA

WEIGHT LIFTER

MADE DEBUT AT AGE OF TWO WHEN HE USED
PEDIATRICIAN FOR SNATCH AND PRESS, 1945.
LIFTED 331-POUND WEIGHT AND HELD IT
ABOVE HEAD FOR FIVE SECONDS DESPITE
PRESENCE OF LIVE WASP IN TRUNKS, 1962.
RETIRED AFTER ATTAINING U.S. TITLE, 1966
WORLD CHAMPIONSHIP, 1967
DOUBLE HERNIA, 1968.

YOU CAN SEE
SHE'S NOT
A
BASEBALL FAN

IF TV SPORTS COVERED A FAMILY QUARREL

At 5 foot 10 and a beer-bloated 195 pounds, **Waldo Wiltfang** combines a **vile temper** with a **fearless disregard for civility!** A high-school drop-out and a Marine Corps reject, he will be **tough to stop,** especially in the late going, when he has a tendency to become **deranged!**

Here we see Wilma sneak up behind Waldo and break a **bridge chair over his head** during a **pre-season clash** earlier this year! Although Waldo suffered a **mild concussion,** the contest was called because of supper! And, naturally, the action didn't count in the standings, which are now tied at **five hospitalizations apiece!**

Back at the Wiltfangs, **Waldo,** fortified by a **fifth of Jack Daniels,** has mounted his **first serious threat** by tearing up Wilma's **charge-a-plates!**

Wilma retaliates with a **$175 dress** she charged this morning, and flaunts it in **Waldo's face!**

Back to live action! Waldo's been **backed deep** into his **own territory,** namely the Wiltfangs' imitation walnut-paneled den! What can he do, Bud?

We've been waiting for Waldo to use the **triple option!** Either to **stand up for his rights** and risk getting his head broken open by a flying vase! To **attempt a reverse** and thus gain time to hide in the cellar! Or to **run straight ahead,** which would be suicide!

Announcements

for

Athletes

Jean-Claude LeDreque
Star Goalie
For The Montreal Canadiens
Hockey Team
Takes Great Pride
In Announcing
The Loss Of His Remaining Tooth
During A Contest
With The New York Rangers
On The Evening
Of Sunday,
The Twelfth Of November
Nineteen Hundred
And Seventy-Two
Madison Square Garden

T. Schuyler Van Grosvenor III
Is Saddened Beyond Belief
To Announce
To His Fellow Members
Of The Southampton Croquet Club
That The Eagerly Awaited
Title Match
With The Northampton Croquet Club
Scheduled For The Afternoon
Of Sunday
The Twenty-Fifth Of June
Nineteen Hundred
And Seventy-Three
Has Been Postponed
Because Of Wicket Rust

Norbert Nugent
Weight-Lifter, Muscleman
And Ardent Physical Culturist
Is Pleased To Announce
That As Of
Saturday, The Seventh Of July,
Nineteen Hundred
And Seventy-Three
He Can Be Considered
The Most Beautiful Thing
On The Beach

Horace "Swimp" Pomerantz
Offensive Guard
For The Minnesota Vikings
Extends His Deepest Regrets
To His Team-Mates
As Well As To The Members
Of The Opposing Team
For Failing To Use
An Effective Deodorant
On Sunday, The Fifth of November
Nineteen Hundred And Seventy-Two

Lance Latouche
Professional Ski Bum
Is Pleased To Announce
That Following
An Incredible Three Days
In The Vicinity
Of Stowe, Vermont
He Has Now Made Out
With At Least One Chick
In Every Major Ski Lodge
On The East Coast

Starting Pitcher
Eldon "Lefty" Scurvy
Of The Detroit Tigers
Having Allowed
Twelve Earned Runs
in Two Innings
To The Milwaukee Brewers
Takes Great Sorrow
In Announcing
The Death
Of His Curve Ball
On Friday,
The Twelfth Of May
Nineteen Hundred
And Seventy-Three

Head Linesman
T. Wilfred Scroon
Wishes To Thank
His Friends And Co-Workers
For Their Letters
Of Sympathy And Condolence
Following
The Swallowing Of His Whistle
During The
Nebraska-Oklahoma
Football Game
On The Twenty-Fifth
Of November
Nineteen Hundred
And Seventy-Two

The Student Body
Of Gribbley Tech
Commemorating The Thirty-Sixth
Consecutive Loss
Of Its Basketball Team
Requests The Pleasure Of Your Company
At The Public Stoning
Of Head Coach
Myron "Hurry-Up" Muldoon
At Three O'Clock On The Afternoon
Of Tuesday, The Fifth Of December
Nineteen Hundred And Seventy-Two
Victory Mall

Elmer E. Esterhazy
Is Pleased To Announce
That He Viewed
Nine Televised Football Games
On The Week-End
Of December First And Second
Nineteen Hundred And Seventy Two

Mrs. Elmer E. Esterhazy
Is Equally Pleased To Announce
The Start Of A Wonderful Affair
With Next-Door Neighbor
Wally Wickwire
On The Week-End
Of December First And Second
Nineteen Hundred And Seventy Two

And now—
a Special Guest Appearance
by Mad's Maddest Artist
DON MARTIN

who now presents

THE
POLAR BEAR CLUB
DIVING
COMPETITION

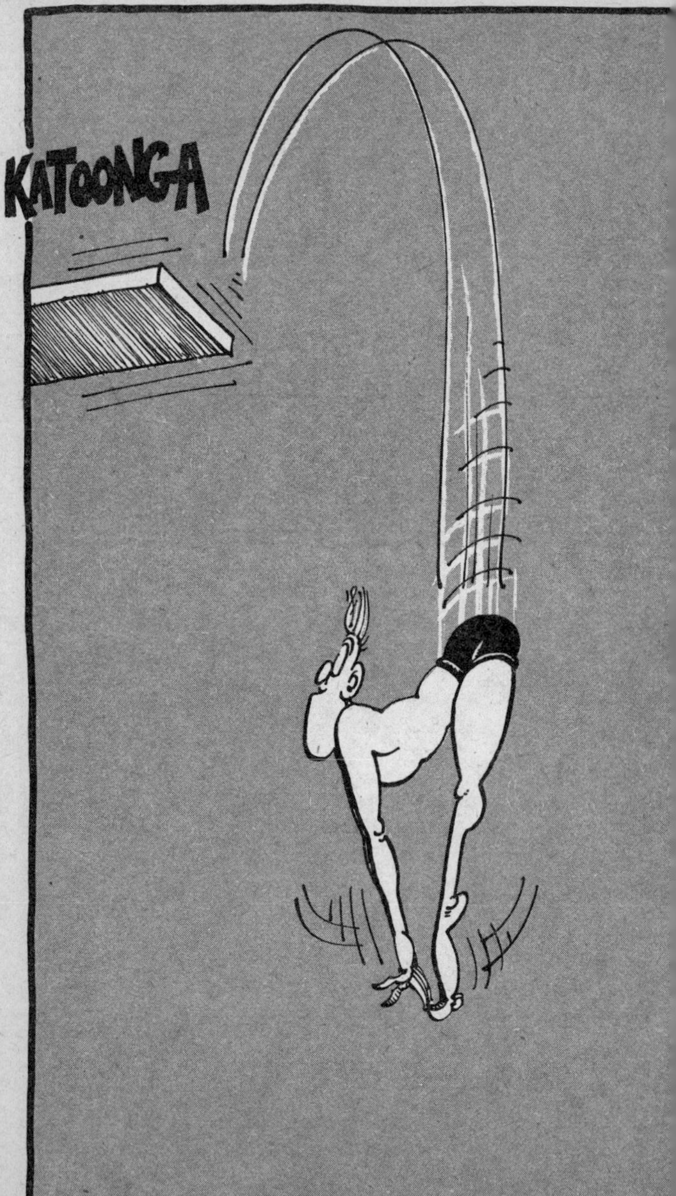
KATOONGA

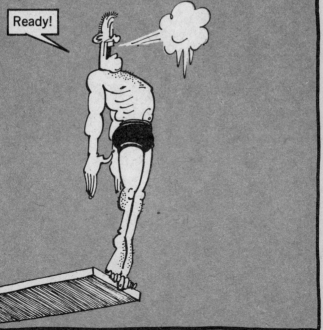

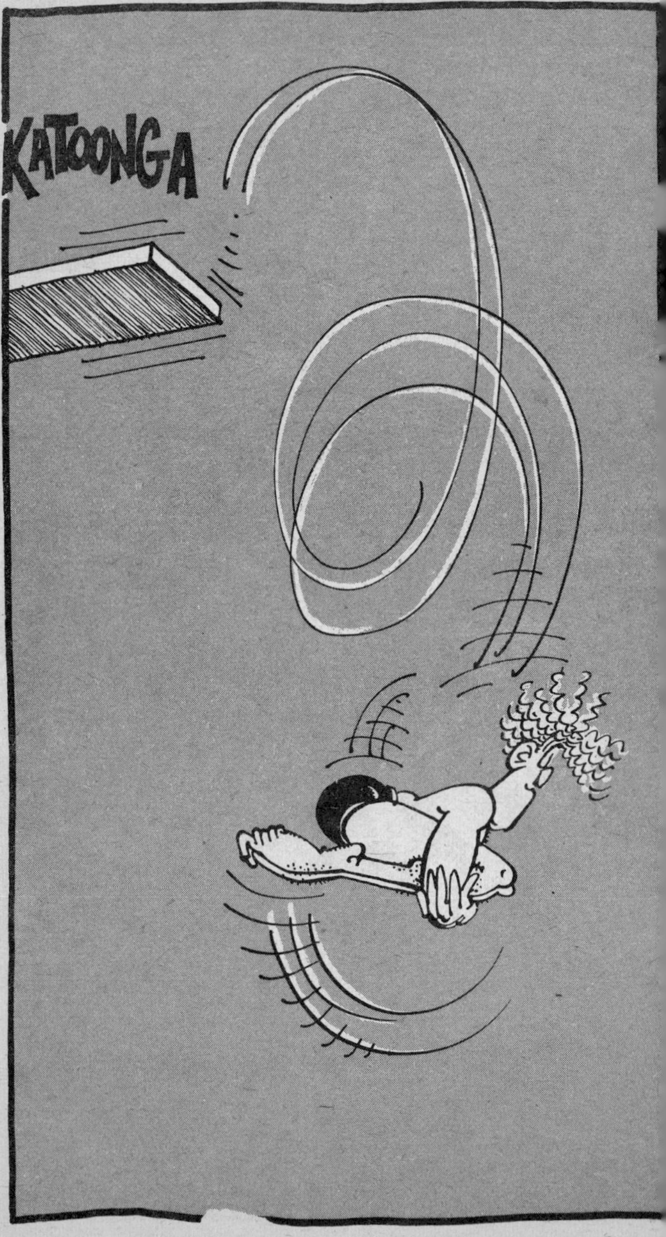
KATOONGA

IF
SPORTS EDITORS
WROTE HEADLINES
FOR
GREAT
HISTORICAL
EVENTS

1200 B.C.

Greek Quick-Opener Stuns Trojans

219 B.C.

Hannibal "At Peak" On Eve of Rome Tilt

44 B.C.

CAESAR LOSES TO BRUTUS IN SUDDEN DEATH PLAY-OFF

215 A.D.

Lions Hungry for Victory As Christian Clash Nears

525 A.D.

ARTHUR SETS JOUST SLATE

Season to Bow with Knight Game

540 A.D.

Galahad Choice to Grab Cup As Race For Grail Begins

1261

MONGOLS PROVE BIG POLO FANS

1431

Joan of Arc Favored In French Stake Race

1512

Michelangelo Credits Good Sistine Showing To Strong Backstroke

1542

HENRY VIII DROPS FIFTH IN A ROW

1697

Pirates Use Hit and Run, Take Flag as Kidd, Mates Divide Winners' Share

1745

Casanova Notches 18th Straight, Credits Success to "Fast Pitch"

1748

BEN FRANKLIN EXTENDS STRING

1769

DE SADE WHIPS FOE, LEADS BY A STROKE

1776

BETSY ROSS SEWS UP FLAG

1781

Redcoat Streak Snapped

Colonists Wrap Up Title at Yorktown As Washington Has Perfect Day

1793

MARIE ANTOINETTE LOSES BY A HEAD

1844

Morse Hits Wire First, Sets New Dash Record

1865

Yanks Edge Rebs As Grant Staggers To Winning Goal

1871

Stanley Trails Livingstone On Eve of Big African Meet

1876

REDSKINS ROUT BLUES, 265-0
Outmanned Custermen Close Out Season In Tilt at Little Big Horn

1895

Marconi Takes to Air, Finds Open Receiver

1899

FREUD GOES DEEP

1919

Wilson Predicts
14-Point Victory
In New League

1927

LINDBURGH
FLIES OUT

THE BIG-TIME ATHLETE
YESTERDAY
and
TODAY

YESTERDAY

TODAY

YESTERDAY

TODAY

YESTERDAY

YESTERDAY

TODStayAY

BAND
FORMATIONS
FOR
SMALL
COLLEGES

A Mad look at the most stirring
half-time displays as performed
by leading small college bands.

The Eastern Ohio College of Business and Finance is famed for its Stock Market Graph Formation, which depicts the memorable Wall Street Crash of 1929.

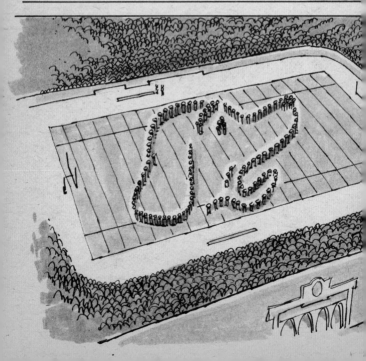

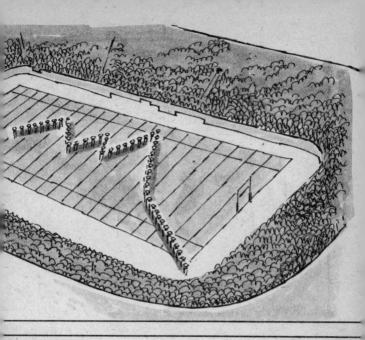

The Missouri School of Veterinarians
steps off its heralded Canine Formation,
which shows a Great Dane with heartburn.

The marching band of the New Jersey
Academy of Magicians pleases its fans
by disappearing in mid-formation.

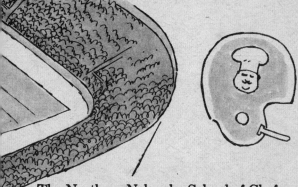

The Northern Nebraska School of Chefs
is proud of its Pasta Formation, which
depicts a serving of cooked spaghetti.

The California Institute of Extremists stuns spectators with its Time-Bomb Formation, which utilizes a real bomb.

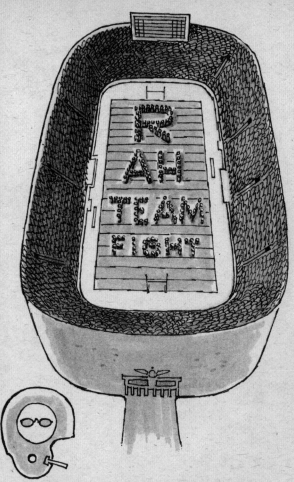

The Iowa College of Optometrists exhorts its team to victory with its famous Eye Chart Formation.

The marching band of the Oklahoma College of Mediums and Spiritualists presents an outline of the school's 1973 commencement speaker, Henry VIII.

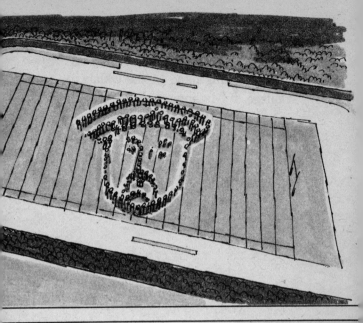

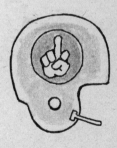

The band of the Michigan School of
Pornography has been forced to censor
last year's most successful formation.

Sports
For Better
Or Verse

You Are Old, Henry Aaron

"You are old, Henry Aaron," the southpaw said,
   "You are no longer able to hit;
"Your swing has no zip and your timing is dead;
   "Don't you think at your age you should quit?"

"You are right," Henry Aaron replied to the youth,
   "That my great slugging days should be through;
"To prove to us both that you utter the truth,
   "Why not pitch me a slider or two?"

"You are old," said the southpaw, approaching the mound,
    "And extinct as the Olduvai Man;
"With luck you will dribble the ball on the ground—
    "If not that, you will certainly fan."

"You are right," Henry Aaron replied, "to recall
    "That I dodder and turn into seed;
"Perhaps I may catch just a piece of the ball,
    "Which would be a great triumph indeed."

"You are old," said the southpaw, his pitch on the way,
   "Of your fate there can be not a doubt;
"And yet you persist in this hopeless display
   "When you know in your heart you are out."

"You are right." Henry Aaron replied. "To my ear
   "There is truth in your every remark;
"But my bat, I discover, is deaf and I fear
   "It has hit the ball out of the park."

Oh TV! My TV!

O TV! My TV!
Our day has just begun
With "Fishing Tips" at 10 a.m.
   And tennis, noon to 1;
And, in between, a hockey game
   On tape from Montreal,
And then the finals, from Duluth,
   Of college volleyball.

O TV! My TV!
Your presence fills my day
With highlights of last season's game
   'Twixt Cleveland and Green Bay;
And, after that, a look in depth
   At Frazier's knock-out punch,
And then a break for local news
   While I prepare my lunch.

O TV! My TV!
I haven't left your side:
At 4 there is a possum hunt—
    Curt Gowdy is our guide;
And then I switch your channels
    To behold an interview
With Cincinnati's Johnny Bench
    And Oakland's Vida Blue.

O TV! My TV!
You next provide the thrill
Of basketball from Luxembourg,
    And skiing from Brazil;
And then to Sweden to observe
    A Frisbee match at night,
Concluded by a rugby game—
    All via satellite.

O TV! My TV!
The night is drawing nigh;
And on your screen a bobsled team
    Of dwarfs is racing by;
And while I bolt my supper down,
    You show at 8:15
A croquet match, then analyze
    The current hopscotch scene.

O TV! My TV!
Our day comes to an end;
'Tis 2 a.m., O faithful pal,
    O most devoted friend;
And as we part, your final words
    I never shall forget—
How fitting that Cosell should preach
    Your late-night Sermonette.

The Sunday Golfer

Under a tree that's in the rough
The Sunday golfer hunts;
His ball is buried in the grass,
And finding it, he grunts:
"I'll give myself a better lie,
"But only just this once."

He tees the ball upon a twig,
  Then shouts a mighty "Fore!"
And swings his club, which moves the ball
  A solid foot or more;
"A practice shot," he mumbles,
  "Which does not affect my score."

He swings again and watches while
    The ball curves in a hook,
Then mutters as it disappears
    Into a muddy brook:
"It's clear the ball was poorly made;
    "This shot I'll overlook."

At last he makes it to the green,
    To where his colleagues are,
Then dribbles in a two-foot putt
    And, lighting a cigar,
Says "What a day I'm having—
    I just made my seventh par."

YOU CAN SEE
SHE'S NOT
A
FOOTBALL FAN

IF
SPORTS EDITORS
WROTE HEADLINES
FOR
THE BIBLE

ADAM, EVE TOP-SEEDED IN EDEN MIXED DOUBLES

Noah Schedules Ark Doubleheader as Flood Poses Threat To Game

SAMSON CRUSHES PHILISTINES
Strongman Shows Surprising Power
Despite Clipping Penalty

Methuselah Kicks Off
After 969-Year Wait

Jonah Predicts "Whale Of a Match," Worries Over Inside Position

DANIEL UNDERDOG IN CAGE TOURNEY

And now, in celebration of Women's Lib, we offer the following chapter, which shows what we soon may see

WHEN WOMEN TAKE PART IN MEN'S PROFESSIONAL SPORTS

In Basketball

1. Before the Game

2. Under the Basket

In Baseball

1. As a Base Runner

2. As a Relief Pitcher

4. As the Manager

In Football

1. As the Head Coach

I think I'll put the flanker **there!** No—on **second thought** he'll look better by the **tight end!** But then where will I put the **wide receiver?** Hmm. Maybe if I put the **center** in front of the **fullback**, nobody will notice our **two unmatching guards!** But that leaves no place for the **left tackle! I know!** We'll **store** him in the basement until we get a **bigger place!**

2. As a Starting Player

4. After the Big Play

5. After the Game